# TINTIN'S TRAVEL DIARIES

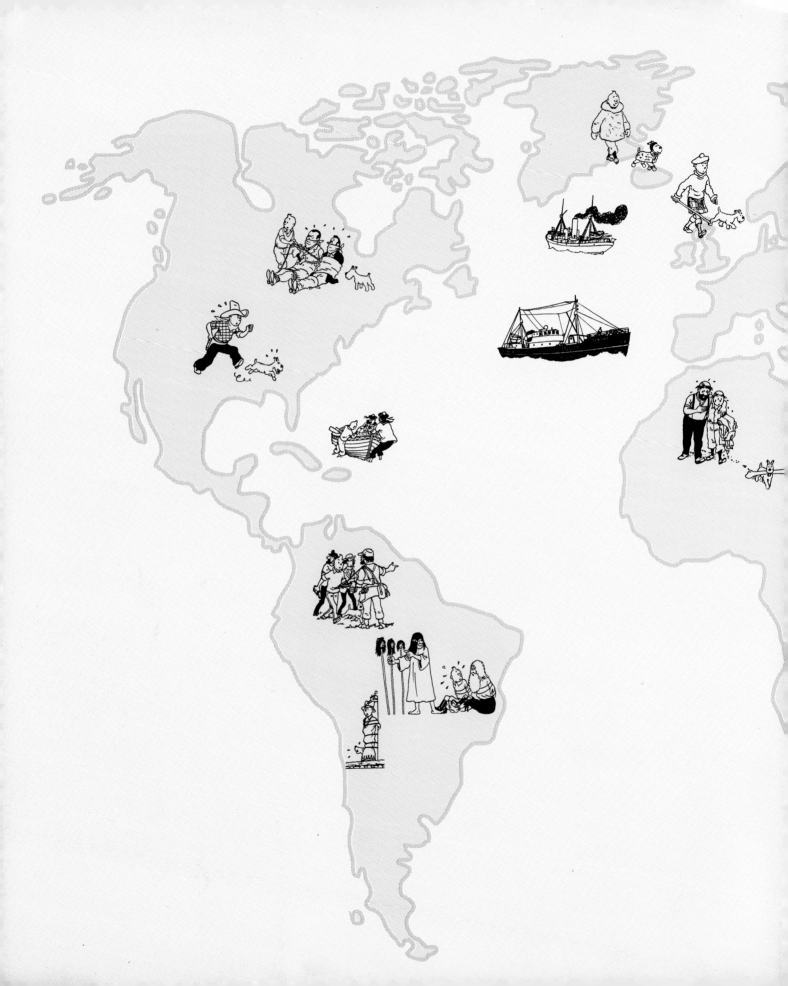

## Publisher's note:

Tintin, the intrepid reporter, first made his appearance January 10, 1929, in a serial newspaper strip with an adventure in the Soviet Union. From there, it was on to the Belgian Congo and then to America. Together with his dog, Snowy; an old seaman, Captain Haddock; an eccentric professor, Cuthbert Calculus; look-alike detectives, Thomson and Thompson; and others, Tintin roamed the world from one adventure to the next.

Tintin's dog, Snowy, a small white fox terrier, converses with Tintin, saves his life many times, and acts as his confidant, despite his weakness for whiskey and a tendency toward greediness. Captain Haddock, in some ways Snowy's counterpart, is a reformed lover of whiskey, with a tendency toward colorful language and a desire to be a gentleman-farmer. Cuthbert Calculus, a hard-of-hearing, sentimental, absent-minded professor, goes from small-time inventor to nuclear physicist. The detectives, Thomson and Thompson, stereotyped characters down to their old-fashioned bowler hats and outdated expressions, are always chasing Tintin. Their attempts at dressing in the costume of the place they are in make them stand out all the more.

The Adventures of Tintin appeared in newspapers and books all over the world. Georges Remi (1907–1983), better known as Hergé, based Tintin's adventures on his own interest in and knowledge of places around the world. The stories were often irreverent, frequently political and satirical, and always exciting and humorous.

Tintin's Travel Diaries is a new series, inspired by Hergé's characters and based on notebooks Tintin may have kept as he traveled. Each book in this series takes the reader to a different country, exploring its geography, and the customs, the culture, and the heritage of the people living there. Hergé's original cartooning is used, juxtaposed with photographs showing the country as it is today, to give a feeling of fun as well as education.

If Hergé's cartoons seem somewhat out of place in today's society, think of the time in which they were drawn. The cartoons reflect the thinking of the day, and set next to modern photographs, we learn something about ourselves and society, as well as about the countries Tintin explores. We can see how attitudes have changed over the course of half a century.

Hergé, himself, would change his stories and drawings periodically to reflect the changes in society and the comments his work would receive. For example, when it was originally written in 1930, Tintin in the Congo, on which Tintin's Travel Diaries: Africa is based, was slanted toward Belgium as the fatherland. When Hergé prepared a color version in 1946, he did away with this slant. Were Hergé alive today, he would probably change many other stereotypes that appear in his work.

From the Congo, Tintin went on to America. This was in 1931. Al Capone was notorious, and the idea of cowboys and Indians, prohibition, the wild west, as well as factories, all held a place of fascination. Cigars of the Pharaoh (1934) introduced Hergé's fans to the mysteries of Egypt and India. A trip to China came with The Blue Lotus in 1936, the first story Hergé thoroughly researched. After that, everything was researched, including revisions of previous stories. The Land of Black Gold, for example, an adventure in the Middle East, was written in 1939, and revised in 1949 and again in 1969.

Although The Broken Ear introduced readers to the Amazon region in 1935, the story was pure fantasy, complete with imaginary countries. In 1974 the adventure continued with Tintin and the Picaros, Hergé's last story. When The Seven Crystal Balls, which was serialized from 1943 to 1944, was continued in 1946, Hergé began to give the reader factual information about pre-Columbian civilization with marginal notes titled "Who were the Incas?" Tintin in the Land of the Soviets was Tintin's first adventure, in 1929, and the only one not to be redone in color.

Tintin's Travel Diaries are fun to read, fun to look at, and provide educational, enjoyable trips around the world. Perhaps, like Tintin, you, too, will be inspired to seek out new adventures!

The publisher particularly wishes to thank Mrs. Christine Ockrent and television channel Antenne 2 for their kind permission to use the title Travel Diaries.

AND THE ANDEAN COUNTRIES

# TINTIN'S TRAVEL DIARIES

A collection conceived and produced by Martine Noblet.

*Les films du sable* thank the following **Connaissance du monde**
*photographers for their participation in this work:*

## Jacques Cornet, Michel Drachoussoff, Gérard Civet, Luc Giard, Alain Mahuzier

*The authors thank C. Erard and
D. De Bruyker for their collaboration.*

First edition for the United States and Canada published
by Barron's Educational Series, Inc., 1995.

All inquiries should be addressed to:
Barron's Educational Series, Inc.
250 Wireless Boulevard
Hauppauge, New York 11788

Library of Congress Catalog Card No. 94-25171

International Standard Book No. 0-8120-6490-9 (hardcover)
International Standard Book No. 0-8120-9161-2 (paperback)

**Library of Congress Cataloging-in-Publication Data**

Deltenre, Chantal.
    Peru and the Andean countries / text by Chantal Deltenre and
Martine Noblet ; translation by Maureen Walker.
        p.   cm. — (Tintin's travel diaries)
    Includes bibliographical references and index.
        ISBN 0-8120-6490-9. — ISBN 0-8120-9161-2 (pbk.)
    1. Peru—Description and travel—Juvenile literature. 2. Andes
Region—Description and travel—Juvenile literature. [1. Peru.
2. Andes Region. 3. Cartoons and comics.] I. Noblet, Martine.
II. Title. III. Series.
F3425.D45   1995
980—dc20                                                94-25171
                                                              CIP
                                                              AC

PRINTED IN HONG KONG
5678    9927    987654321

# PERU
## AND THE ANDEAN COUNTRIES

Text by Chantal Deltenre and Martine Noblet

Translation by Maureen Walker

BARRON'S

In the 1950s, after the turmoil of the Second World War, I made up my mind to set out on a great adventure around the world. I was a sort of early Tintin, full of noble ideas, eager to discover the beauties of our universe.

In my little Citroen, which slowly and peacefully made its way reliably across the deserts and mountain ranges of America, I became an explorer, ready to forget the misfortunes and anxieties that had troubled my childhood.

I felt as much pure joy discovering the great cities of the North as I did the jungles of Central America, but the biggest thrill for me was in Cusco and Machu Picchu, where I felt sure that I was about to discover the treasure of the Inca in their palaces, with gardens filled with golden flowers, just as Hergé had imagined.

Thanks to the reading I had done as a child, and to the little lad with the unruly lock of hair and his dog, Snowy, I achieved the greatest dream imaginable for a lover of the earth, so eager to get to know its inhabitants that I had to make the trip.

JACQUES CORNET

When I was traveling through the Andean *cordillera*, my traveling companion kept saying: "It's amazing! This is pure Tintin! Look, it's exactly the same! When I get back to Paris, I'm going to have my Tintin books bound in leather, with the page-edges gold-leafed—it'll be the best travel souvenir I could think of." I think the *Temple of the Sun* is among the best of them because of its accuracy in pinpointing the places where events took place, a part of the world that has been most successful in preserving its setting and traditions in the face of growing planet-wide uniformity.

The Andean *cordillera* is a fortress raised against outside influences and invasions, protected in the east by the terrible green hell of the Amazon region, and in the west by steep ramparts where people, whose lives are still untouched by our times, have taken refuge.

To write this introduction, I went back to my old copy of the *Temple of the Sun*, with its worn pages and dog-eared corners. Rereading Tintin brought back to me not only childhood joys and memories but my travels in Peru and Bolivia, with all the aromas, feelings, and wonderment I experienced during my stay there. This book makes it possible to experience a unique journey in the land of the Inca, a journey more true, more moving, and even more exciting than a whole expedition.

GÉRARD CIVET

# CONTENTS

**1.** WHY ARE THE ANDES CALLED A "CORDILLERA"?                           10

**2.** WHICH IS THE LARGEST RAPTOR?                                        12

**3.** WHAT IS THE MYSTERY OF THE NAZCA?                                   14

**4.** WHERE DID THE ANDEAN INDIANS COME FROM?                             16

**5.** WERE THE RULING INCA PEACEFUL?                                      18

**6.** HOW DID THE INCA PRESERVE THEIR DEAD?                               20

**7.** WHAT CITY WAS NICKNAMED THE "NAVEL OF THE WORLD"?                   22

**8.** WHERE IS MACHU PICCHU?                                             24

**9.** HOW DID THE INCA TRAVEL?                                           26

**10.** DID THE INCA WRITE?                                               28

**11.** WHO WERE THE CONQUISTADORES?                                      30

**12.** DOES THE TEMPLE OF THE SUN STILL EXIST?                           32

**13.** WHAT BECAME OF THE INDIANS' GODS?                                 34

**14.** WHO LIVES IN THE ANDES TODAY?                                     36

**15.** WHAT IS LIFE LIKE IN AN ANDEAN VILLAGE?                           38

**16.** WHAT MATERIAL ARE PONCHOS MADE OF?                                40

**17.** WHAT IS THE ANDEAN FLUTE CALLED?                                  42

**18.** WHAT IS GUANO USED FOR?                                           44

**19.** WHAT IS KNOWN AS "EL NIÑO"?                                       46

**20.** WHERE DID POTATOES COME FROM?                                     48

**21.** IN WHICH COUNTRY IS "SUCRE" THE MAIN CURRENCY UNIT?               50

**22.** WHERE WAS "EL DORADO"?                                            52

**23.** WHAT IS COCA?                                                     54

**24.** WHAT ARE REEDS FROM LAKE TITICACA USED FOR?                       56

**25.** HOW DID BOLIVIA GET ITS NAME?                                     58

**26.** WHERE IS THE "RICH HILL"?                                         60

**27.** WHICH IS THE MOST STRIKING OF ALL DESERTS?                        62

**28.** WHICH IS THE WORLD'S LONGEST COUNTRY?                             64

**29.** HOW DID THE GALAPAGOS ISLANDS GET THEIR NAME?                     66

**30.** WHERE DID THE GIANT STATUES ON EASTER ISLAND COME FROM?           68

GLOSSARY                                                                 70

CHRONOLOGICAL CHART                                                      72

MAP                                                                      73

INDEX                                                                    74

BIBLIOGRAPHY: PERU AND THE ANDEAN COUNTRIES,
FOR READERS FROM 7 TO 77                                                 75

The words in **boldface** are found in the glossary on page 70.

# WHY ARE THE ANDES CALLED A "CORDILLERA"?

The Andes form the backbone of South America, running alongside the Pacific coast for 4,500 miles (7,200 km). They consist of narrow parallel mountain chains; called "cordilleras" in Spanish.

These young mountains with their jagged tops are partly volcanic in origin. From north to south they stretch from Panama and Venezuela to Cape Horn, passing through Colombia, Ecuador, Peru, Bolivia, and Argentina on the way. Among them rise the highest summits in the world, after those in Asia. Aconcagua, in Argentina, reaches 22,831 feet (6,959 m), and its neighbor, Fitz Roy, is attractive to climbers because of its tall outline and dizzying peak.

The cordilleras, which can be crossed through passes sometimes as high as 15,800 feet (4,816 m), before the development of aviation formed a barrier that divided the South American continent into two parts: to the east, the humid forests of the Amazon region and the grasslands of the pampas; to the west, a narrow coastal area where the climate is often very dry, trapped but also sheltered between the mountains (the sierra) and the Pacific Ocean.

The mountainous plateau of the Andes is so young that in places it is still rising. Some peaks still being formed are volcanoes, like Cotopaxi in Ecuador, with a height of 19,347 feet (5,897 m). The Andean region is subjected to fairly regular tsunamis of **seismic** origin, and to disastrous volcanic eruptions. One in 1985 triggered a mudslide that destroyed the town of Armero in Colombia, and caused the deaths of over 23,000 people.

Top: The Cordilleras    Bottom: The Chicon, 18,040 feet (5,500 m), eastern Cordilleras

# WHICH IS THE LARGEST RAPTOR?

The Andes condor is a very large vulture. Its nearly ten-foot wingspan and magnificent black plumage, fringed with white on the wings, make it king of the sierra.

ondors live in flocks on the tops of the Andes. Like all raptors, these giant birds are scavengers. They feed on dead animals left by the two great carnivores of the Andes, the puma and the jaguar. The puma tends to hunt at high altitude, whereas its cousin the jaguar is lord of the dense humid forests that cover the Andean valleys. The jaguar's favorite prey is the peccary, a small wild pig. But it does not overlook the great **anteater**, either, or the howler monkeys, which keep up a ceaseless din with parrots of all types.

On the **puna**, the grassy heathland that covers the high plains at altitudes over 10,000 feet (3,000 m), and on the slopes of the sierra, the absence of trees favors very different kinds of fauna. The vicuña and the guanaco, wild cousins of the llama, are found there. They live in company with a small ostrich, called the nandu, and two species of rodents typical of this area, the viscache, or "American hare," and the **chinchilla**, now decimated because of its very fine, much sought-after fur. The cavy, or guinea pig, is the ancestor of the guinea pig we know today. Like the rabbit in Europe, it was long ago domesticated by the Indians. Its delicate meat provides the inhabitants of the sierra with their favorite festival dish.

Top: Large Andean bird of prey
Bottom: A young Bolivian

# WHAT IS THE MYSTERY OF THE NAZCA?

Around 1930, while flying over the Nazca plain, aviators noticed strange "lines" forming pictures of animals or geometric shapes, some nearly 5,000 feet (1,500 m) long.

In 1939, the archeologist Paul Kosok discovered that the Nazca drawings were the remains of one of Peru's most ancient civilizations.

These designs, named "geoglyphs," date from about 200 B.C. They were laid out using the stones that littered the sandy soil. Depicting plants, birds, lizards, or monkeys, they look only like pathways at ground level. The people who made them were probably never able to "see" their drawings, since you have to be high up to put together the whole picture. We don't know how the people of Nazca managed to design and execute these figures. Maybe they were intended for their gods, who could see them from up in the sky. Another theory is that the entire Nazca plain functioned as an **astronomical** calendar. The day the sun or one of the planets rose in alignment with a drawing marked the beginning of sowing, field irrigation, or harvesting.

From these distant predecessors of the **Inca** there remain some handsome vases painted with religious themes, woven items, and ruins of a great city, Cahuacchi.

The geoglyphics at Nazca

# WHERE DID THE ANDEAN INDIANS COME FROM?

The Amerindians, who came from Asia over 20,000 years ago, before the Bering Strait separated Siberia and Alaska, took several thousand years to occupy all of America and to found civilizations there.

About 2500 B.C., the ancestors of the Peruvians and the Mexicans discovered how to cultivate corn, which became the staple food of all the so-called **pre-Columbian** people. In Mexico, too, less than 3,000 years ago, the Olmec, distant predecessors of the Maya and the **Aztec**, founded the first great civilization on the American continent.

But other civilizations flourished at the foot of the Andes. The **Chavin**, who were skillful craftsmen, settled in Peru. The **Paraca** were expert weavers, and the **Mochica** astounding potters and designers whose works retain a lingering charm. The **Chimu** worshipped the moon-goddess. Around the eleventh century, these excellent goldsmiths built a capital, Chanchan, whose ruins cover eight square miles (20 sq. km) near the Peruvian coast. The most fascinating of all the pre-Columbian civilizations, however, is still that of the Inca, the founders of Cusco. Alas, these great conquerors had barely a century to establish their magnificent culture before the empire was devastated by a bloody **conquistador**, the Spaniard **Pizarro**.

Top: A Varayoc Peruvian in Cuzco
Bottom left: A Bolivian woman in the Charazani Valley
Bottom right: A Peruvian woman in holiday costume

# WERE THE RULING INCA PEACEFUL?

From 1438 to 1532, the brief period of the Inca was mainly a long series of military conquests. The expansion of the empire began with Pachacutec, king of Cusco...

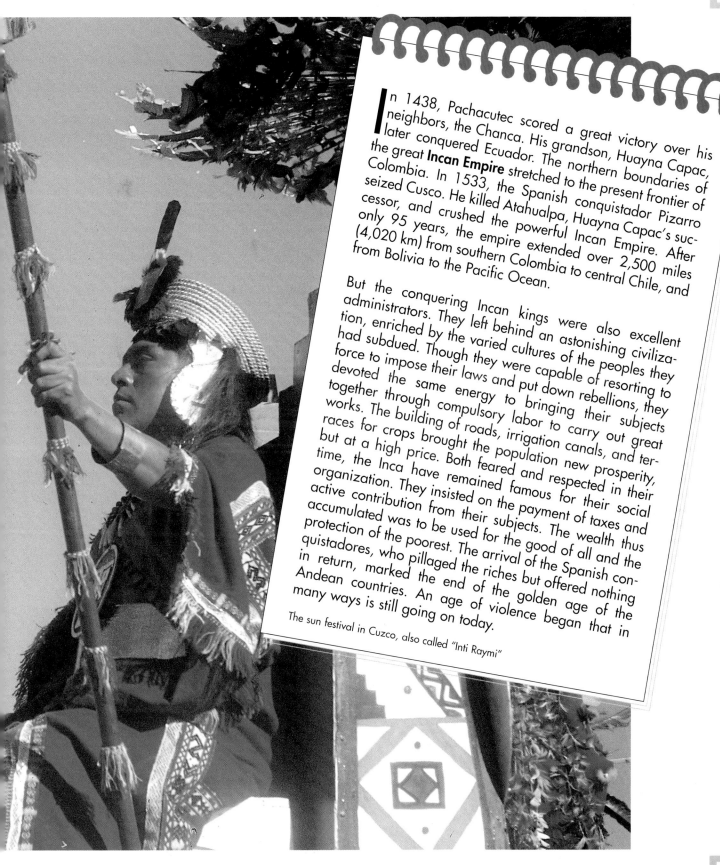

In 1438, Pachacutec scored a great victory over his neighbors, the Chanca. His grandson, Huayna Capac, later conquered Ecuador. The northern boundaries of the great **Incan Empire** stretched to the present frontier of Colombia. In 1533, the Spanish conquistador Pizarro seized Cusco. He killed Atahualpa, Huayna Capac's successor, and crushed the powerful Incan Empire. After only 95 years, the empire extended over 2,500 miles (4,020 km) from southern Colombia to central Chile, and from Bolivia to the Pacific Ocean.

But the conquering Incan kings were also excellent administrators. They left behind an astonishing civilization, enriched by the varied cultures of the peoples they had subdued. Though they were capable of resorting to force to impose their laws and put down rebellions, they devoted the same energy to bringing their subjects together through compulsory labor to carry out great works. The building of roads, irrigation canals, and terraces for crops brought the population new prosperity, but at a high price. Both feared and respected in their time, the Inca have remained famous for their social organization. They insisted on the payment of taxes and active contribution from their subjects. The wealth thus accumulated was to be used for the good of all and the protection of the poorest. The arrival of the Spanish conquistadores, who pillaged the riches but offered nothing in return, marked the end of the golden age of the Andean countries. An age of violence began that in many ways is still going on today.

The sun festival in Cuzco, also called "Inti Raymi"

# HOW DID THE INCA PRESERVE THEIR DEAD?

The Inca customarily embalmed their dead and wrapped them in several shrouds. They then placed them in the bottom of a cave or pit and covered them with a huge mound. Important people were buried above ground in stone chambers.

Like the Egyptians, the Inca preserved their dead with the utmost care, but that is not the only resemblance between these two civilizations. The supreme god of the **Quechua** ruling family was the sun god, Inti. Again like the Egyptians, the Quechua worshipped the moon, stars, thunder, and rainbow as attributes of their supreme god, **Viracocha**. The cult of the earth-mother, Pachamama, even older than the Incan religion, had remained firmly rooted among the common people, who were more superstitious than the nobility. Stones were revered in various forms: aeroliths fallen from space, the emerald, or especially the bezoar, a "stone" formed in the stomach of the llama.

Each home was placed under the protection of conopas, gods represented by small statues of people or animals. Various rites honored all things huaca, which means "sacred." This included a temple, a mountain, a spring, a river, or merely a snake or a flower.

The priests of the temples, who were both wise men and teachers, along with "chosen women" dedicated to the sun-god, were a separate class in Quechua society.

Top: The sun festival in Cuzco
Bottom: A mummy found in the desert near Nazca

# WHAT CITY WAS NICKNAMED THE "NAVEL OF THE WORLD"?

*Founded at the beginning of the thirteenth century, Cusco was the Incan capital city. Its name means "Navel of the World" in the Quechua language.*

Located in the Andes, at an altitude of 11,200 feet (3,400 m), Incan country still displays the genius of its builders, despite destruction and looting by conquistadores and later by missionaries. Though the latter built cathedrals and convents over the finest temples and palaces in Cusco, they did not succeed in eliminating them entirely or in changing the majestic sanctuary of Sacsahuaman, which still dominates the city.

In the fifteenth century, Emperor Pachacutec transformed the little town of Cusco, made of wood and thatch, into a grandiose city of stone, which made a keen impression on the Spaniards. From the capital at Cusco to the city of **Machu Picchu**, the Incan civilization owes its greatest glory to its architects.

Incan architecture relied mainly on the art of the stone masons. The blocks fit into each other with such accuracy that mortar was unnecessary. Using only stone tools to cut the granite and limestone, the stonecutters reshaped each stone many times by putting it in place, then lifting it out, carving and replacing it until it fit perfectly. Walls, roads on steep slopes, and **aqueducts** built this way—their precision still amazing today—have withstood all seismic activity. The whole population helped to move the blocks of stone, some weighing over 100 metric tons. The Incas were aware of the disc, which they considered to be the sacred image of the sun, but they knew nothing of the wheel, so transportation was accomplished by the strength of men's arms, or by llamas.

Left: The fortress at Sacsahuaman     Right: Machu Picchu

# WHERE IS MACHU PICCHU?

Just before the Spanish conquest, the Inca erected the most fantastic of their monuments, Machu Picchu. They located it northwest of Cusco at an altitude of over 8,000 feet (2,400 m).

In 1911, the explorer **Hiram Bingham** discovered the narrow trail, abandoned for nearly four centuries, that led to this exceptional site. Described as the "eighth wonder of the world," and a tribute to the artistry of its Peruvian builders, the city overlooks an impassable gorge at the base of the sugarloaf-shaped peak.

With its temples, palaces, city walls, and extraordinary architecture of terraces clinging to the mountain, Machu Picchu suddenly became legend. Its ruins include nearly 300 stone buildings. Farming families lived in one-room houses grouped around a central courtyard. A stone **aqueduct** conducted water from mountain streams through a network of canals and basins to the city and down to cultivated terraces on the lower slopes.

Abandoned and forgotten after the collapse of the Incan Empire and thereby preserved from pillaging by the Spaniards, Machu Picchu seems almost intact amid the mountains. The city still seems haunted by the Inca, despite crowds of tourists who come to admire it.

The ruins of the city at Machu Picchu

# HOW DID THE INCA TRAVEL?

**9**

The Incan Empire was crisscrossed with paved roads, sometimes more than 1,250 miles (2,012 km) long. Mountains were navigated by means of bridges, tunnels, or winding flights of stairs.

Roads were strategic highways for soldiers setting off to conquer new territories or put down revolts, but they also made it possible to move populations. Indeed, the Inca used to deport the inhabitants of regions that they had just conquered and replace them with faithful Quechua subjects.

Runners who relayed each other every mile and a quarter provided high-speed transmission of news from the provinces and orders from the Incan ruler . . . or brought him freshly caught fish from the coast.

Since the Inca did not use the wheel, goods were carried on the backs of people or animals, with stops at cookhouses that were like inns. Some carefully paved highways rank among the masterpieces of Incan civilization. Mountains and streams were crossed on strong rope bridges suspended over empty space, an Incan invention. One of them, 146 feet (44.5 m) long, still straddles the Apurimac River.

Top: A rope suspension bridge
Bottom left: Stone steps from the Incas
Bottom right: A caravan of llamas

# DID THE INCA WRITE?

The Inca were unaware of writing. The quipu, a colored woolen cord with knots of various lengths, helped them keep track of their administrative accounting.

The Incan people passed on complex ideas by oral tradition, particularly on astronomy. For the Quechua, the stars were the manifestation of the gods, and the priests were masters in the art of star-gazing. From their observations, they deduced not only omens but also an exact calendar for working in the fields.

Quechua physicians were able to cure a wide range of diseases using the medicinal plants of the sierra, which were sold from village to village by itinerant pharmacists. Western medicine has adopted a number of their remedies: cocaine, derived from the tonic leaves of the coca, and quinine or quinquina, an excellent remedy for fevers.

The Quechua were innovative farmers, too. We adopted the use of **guano** as a fertilizer from them, as well as many edible plants, including the potato, which later saved many Europeans from starvation. Today, agronomists are rediscovering certain cereals specially selected for growing at very high altitudes, like quinoa, which is high in protein. The Quechua also perfected useful ways to control harmful insects and preserve food.

Top: Quipu
Bottom: Remains of the Incan circular tower at Sacsahuaman

# WHO WERE THE CONQUISTADORES?

Cortes, the conqueror of Mexico, and Pizarro, conqueror of Peru, are the most famous of the conquistadores, generals to whom the kings of Spain entrusted the task of subduing the New World and seizing its gold.

For the kings of Spain, the Americas evoked the old legends of **El Dorado**, "the country where the streets are paved with gold." The conquistadores, usually belonging to the gentry of the impoverished province of Estremadura, were excited about the conquest, which they saw as a unique opportunity for glory and fortune.

As **Hernando Cortés** had been welcomed to the shores of Mexico by **Aztecs** adorned with rich jewels, Pizarro in his turn was convinced that the Incan Empire would also be overflowing with treasure. But the land of the Quechua was not very rich in precious metals. Such gold as the Inca had, they either wore or used to decorate temples dedicated to the supreme god, the sun, for the yellow metal mirrored its brilliance. The Inca never thought of minting money, much less of shutting it up in chests.

But the conquistadores, blinded by the lure of gain and knowing nothing of Quechua customs, rushed after the much over-rated treasures. As in the case of the Aztec, the apparent splendor of the Inca caused their downfall. Five years after Pizarro's landing, the powerful empire of Peru, devastated, looted, and dominated by a few greedy and pitiless invaders, was reduced to nothing but ruins.

Left: Gold museum in Bogota
Right: Statue of Pizarro

# DOES THE TEMPLE OF THE SUN STILL EXIST?

Like all the splendid buildings in Cusco, the Temple of the Sun was razed after Pizarro's brutal conquest of Peru and the forced conversion of the Quechua to Christianity.

**S**mallpox, a disease common among the Spanish but unknown to the Inca, turned out to be a weighty ally for Pizarro. From the time of his first landing in 1527, it spread throughout Peru like wildfire, carrying off Emperor Huayna Capac and inciting a long war of succession between his sons Huascar and Atahualpa. Returning five years later with barely 200 soldiers, Pizarro easily invaded an empire undermined by illness and civil war. He seized Atahualpa, who had come to meet him with 20,000 men, and held him prisoner for nine months before having him strangled on August 29, 1533.

Pizarro and his men then pillaged Incan treasure and ransacked the remnants of their power, while the priests had the temples demolished to erect churches, at the same time baptizing the Indians by force. The Indians, deprived of their lands for the benefit of Spanish colonists and reduced to forced labor in mines and on plantations, struggled for a long time against the ill-treatment inflicted by the conquistadores. The king of Spain himself was upset about it, but the repression remained harsh.

Even today, the Quechua remember this terrible time and feel the effects of its injustice. They are aware of their proud past, which they believe must be honored.

The Convent of Santo Domingo at Cuzco, built on top of the remains of the Incan sun temple

# WHAT BECAME OF THE INDIANS' GODS?

*Fiercely prohibited by the Christian missionaries who had come from Spain with the conquistadores, the traditional religion of the Indians endured in secret or merged with Christian festivals and ceremonies.*

The priests, and the Jesuits in particular, tried to destroy any object that was a reminder of a religion they deemed idolatrous: festival cloth, feather adornments, and sacred conch shells were forcibly replaced by rosaries and religious pictures. Temples were devastated as were various places venerated by the Indians. Monuments, mountain tops, springs, rivers, or rocks were topped by Christian crosses.

However, the Indians managed to preserve their ancestral beliefs. Christ was often identified with Viracocha, the Incan creator-god, and the Virgin Mary with the earth goddess. In their honor, in many villages rites are celebrated that used to take place in the ancient temples. On festival days, statues of Christian saints are carried in procession just as emblems of the pagan gods were carried in the past. Finally, the annual carnival, a festival in which anything goes, gives the Indians the opportunity to renew their ties with the spirits that used to protect them from demons and disease.

In Bolivia, during the festival of Corpus Christi, dancers adorn themselves with condor feathers to capture the sacred bird's legendary strength. In Peru, the bird is tied to the back of a bull that it must bring down. This cruel fight recalls the sacrifices of former times, and for some people symbolizes the victory of the condor, emblem of the Indians, over the Spanish bull.

The sun festival in Cuzco

# WHO LIVES IN THE ANDES TODAY?

*Decimated by massacres, disease, and poverty, the Indians of the Andean countries are only a minority now compared to descendants of the Spanish colonists and people of mixed racial heritage.*

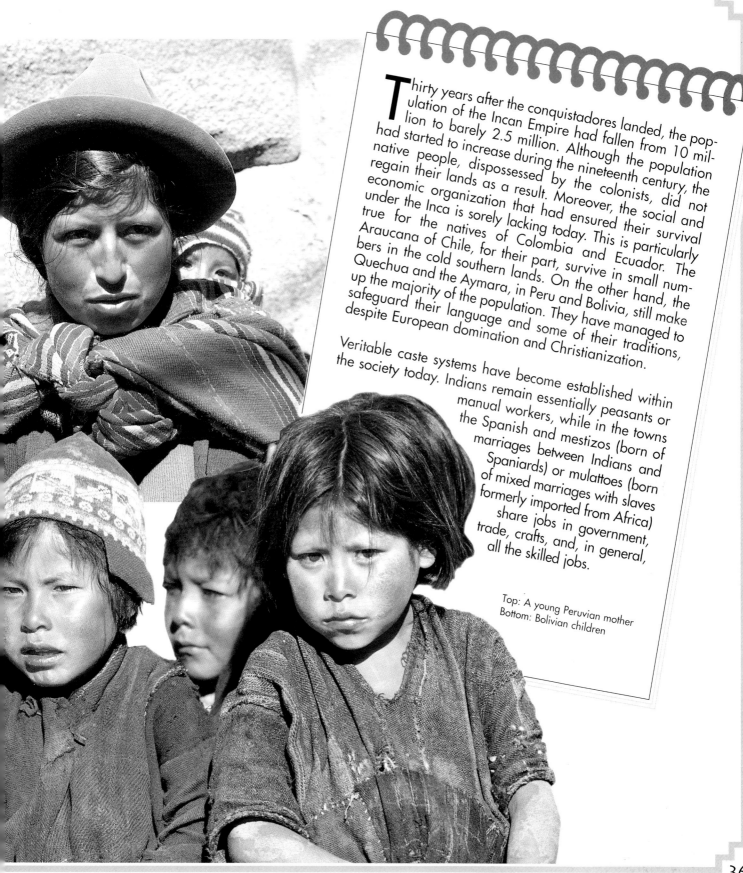

Thirty years after the conquistadores landed, the population of the Incan Empire had fallen from 10 million to barely 2.5 million. Although the population had started to increase during the nineteenth century, the native people, dispossessed by the colonists, did not regain their lands as a result. Moreover, the social and economic organization that had ensured their survival under the Inca is sorely lacking today. This is particularly true for the natives of Colombia and Ecuador. The Araucana of Chile, for their part, survive in small numbers in the cold southern lands. On the other hand, the Quechua and the Aymara, in Peru and Bolivia, still make up the majority of the population. They have managed to safeguard their language and some of their traditions, despite European domination and Christianization.

Veritable caste systems have become established within the society today. Indians remain essentially peasants or manual workers, while in the towns the Spanish and mestizos (born of marriages between Indians and Spaniards) or mulattoes (born of mixed marriages with slaves formerly imported from Africa) share jobs in government, trade, crafts, and, in general, all the skilled jobs.

Top: A young Peruvian mother
Bottom: Bolivian children

# WHAT IS LIFE LIKE IN AN ANDEAN VILLAGE?

On the high mountains of the Andes, cold and lack of oxygen slow down the pace of life. Perhaps that is why the life-style has hardly changed since Incan times.

ouses are always built using traditional materials like stone, rushes, and adobe, a sun-dried clay brick. In the highlands of Peru, thatched roofs are covered with grass in the same manner as Incan homes. The higher the altitude, the less life has changed: where barley or wheat, imported from Europe, or even corn, will not grow, potatoes are still a subsistence food for the Indians. Every village grows its own variety—pink, black, or purple—sometimes hardly bigger than a cherry. Today, sheep are raised for meat and wool, and mules for transportation. But the customs of llama caravans, alpaca wool, and dishes prepared from guinea-pig meat still exist as well.

In the markets, the inhabitants, who come from areas at various altitudes, exchange the fruits and vegetables native to their region. Each community manufactures tools, pottery, and other crafts products, decorated according to its own traditions. The women, wearing costumes and hats typical of their villages, carry goods on their backs in mantas, large pieces of fabric tied around their shoulders.

Left: Preparing *chicha*, alcohol made from wheat
Right: Bolivian village in the Altiplano

# WHAT MATERIAL ARE PONCHOS MADE OF?

Alpaca, vicuña, llama wool, and now lambswool, unknown until the arrival of the Spanish, are always used to weave the "polleras," or layered skirts, of Indian women.

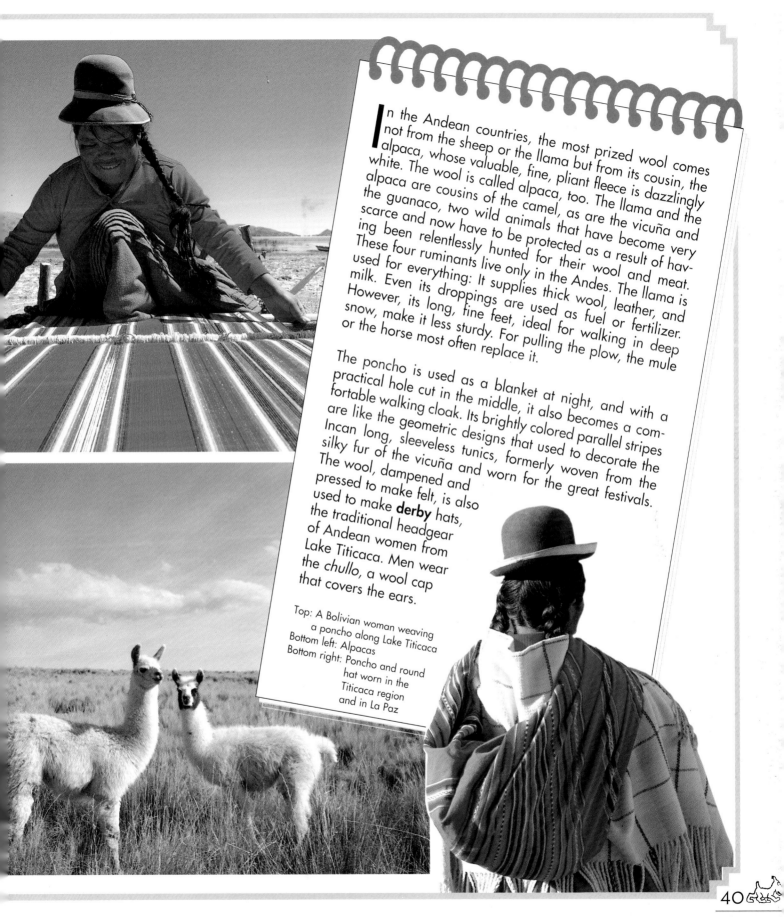

In the Andean countries, the most prized wool comes not from the sheep or the llama but from its cousin, the alpaca, whose valuable, fine, pliant fleece is dazzlingly white. The wool is called alpaca, too. The llama and the alpaca are cousins of the camel, as are the vicuña and the guanaco, two wild animals that have become very scarce and now have to be protected as a result of having been relentlessly hunted for their wool and meat. These four ruminants live only in the Andes. The llama is used for everything: It supplies thick wool, leather, and milk. Even its droppings are used as fuel or fertilizer. However, its long, fine feet, ideal for walking in deep snow, make it less sturdy. For pulling the plow, the mule or the horse most often replace it.

The poncho is used as a blanket at night, and with a practical hole cut in the middle, it also becomes a comfortable walking cloak. Its brightly colored parallel stripes are like the geometric designs that used to decorate the Incan long, sleeveless tunics, formerly woven from the silky fur of the vicuña and worn for the great festivals. The wool, dampened and pressed to make felt, is also used to make **derby** hats, the traditional headgear of Andean women from Lake Titicaca. Men wear the *chullo*, a wool cap that covers the ears.

Top: A Bolivian woman weaving a poncho along Lake Titicaca
Bottom left: Alpacas
Bottom right: Poncho and round hat worn in the Titicaca region and in La Paz

# WHAT IS THE ANDEAN FLUTE CALLED?

Along with the drum, the flute is the principal musical instrument of the Andean Indians. But the famous "kena" is just one of many models.

Like poncho designs, the shapes of felt hats, or patterns on pottery, Andean music varies from one people to another, and even from one village to another. Indeed, in each region, dances, songs, and characteristic instruments are passed on from one generation to the next.

Borrowed from the Spanish, the guitar, the harp, and the charango, a small guitar with a case made from **armadillo** shell, are usually all made in the same way. There are hundreds of different models of flutes, drums, and horns, however, that are played solo or in bands, at home, or in the streets during carnival.

Dances and songs, called *huaynos*, sometimes romantic, sometimes frenzied, existed in Incan times. They are performed today in the same way, with dancers disguised as jaguars, bears, condors, or warriors. Traditions remain lively, and some mountain dances, created after the conquest, make fun of the manners of the Spaniards or their black slaves. In Bolivia, the dance of the Inca commemorates the terrible confrontation between the Incan Emperor Atahualpa and the conquistador Pizarro.

Left: A man playing the "kena" during a festival in Bolivia
Right: A man playing a flute

42

# WHAT IS GUANO USED FOR?

Guano consists of the droppings of seabirds, accumulated in huge deposits on the islands along the coast of Peru. Rich in nitrogen, it was the main fertilizer used by the Inca.

Like sugar and cotton, guano is still one of Peru's essential resources. For a long time it was exported to Europe, before the discovery of chemical fertilizers. But after the Second World War the fall in the price of these products plunged the country into economic crisis. The phenomenon became even worse during the 1960s. Impoverished peasants, most of them Indians, who came from the mountains to look for work on the haciendas or the large plantations on the coast, were once again left without work or resources.

Peru then turned to the fish-bearing waters of the Pacific Ocean, exporting fish meal as cattle fodder.

Though some peasants were able to find jobs in industrial fisheries, others flocked to Lima, the great city that replaced Cusco as the capital of Peru. Nearly one-third of the 23 million Peruvians live there today. The country has few industries. It cannot find work for all the man-power pouring down from the sierra and crowding into shantytowns that are often without sewers, running water, and electricity. Defective sanitary conditions are the underlying cause of terrible **cholera** epidemics that decimate the population of these disadvantaged districts.

Top: Guano
Bottom: Gathering the guano in Peru to use for fertilizer.

# WHAT IS KNOWN AS "EL NIÑO"?

Some summers, a warm ocean current causes the disappearance of Peruvian fishermen's main resource—anchovies! This remarkable event is called "El Niño."

About every four or five years, a warm ocean current moves down from the equatorial zone and flows between the Peruvian coast and the rather cool fish-bearing waters that wash its shores.

The warmer water causes the anchovies to go away, which puts the fishermen in a precarious situation. Indeed, overly intensive fishing, and the lack of modern ships that would allow deep-water fishing, severely handicap the Peruvian fishing industry.

But the climate of Peru has some other curious aspects. Though it rains very rarely on the coast, a padding of mist and drizzle, the garua, caused by cold water currents that normally flow along the coast, frequently obscures the sun during the six winter months.

When the low, whitish sky clears at last, the people of Lima rush to the beaches. But also at this time of year the wind brings a little humid air from the Amazon region across the Andes sierra, and suddenly this desert region is drowned in catastrophic downpours of water.

Top: An old barge in the bay of Paracas
Bottom left: Return of the fish in a small village near Pisco
Bottom right: A sardine cannery in Lima

# 20

# WHERE DID POTATOES COME FROM?

Like many other plants that we think have always been around us, the white potato, a native of the Peruvian sierra, did not exist in Europe before 1492.

otatoes were grown communally, and the surplus was given to those who had less. The harvest was buried during the winter, preserving potatoes as naturally freeze-dried, centuries before the industrial process was invented.

The staple food of the Quechua, and of Amerindians in general, however, was not the potato but corn, the kernel of which was dried, then ground into meal and eaten as flat cakes or gruel. Today corn grows on every continent and is eaten around the world, just like beans, tomatoes, and peanuts, also natives of the Americas. Chocolate, too, is made from the beans of an American tree, the cacao. The Europeans discovered many exotic fruits in the Andes: among them the avocado, pineapple, guava, and papaya, the last two being Incan favorites.

All these plants are still grown today in Andean countries. But sugar and coffee, two plants from the Old World, are now the basis of agricultural wealth. Profits go to the big landowners who have the best land and to the foreign companies handling marketing. Sugarcane is an industrial crop in Peru and Colombia, which, along with Brazil, is also the world's largest producer of coffee.

Left: Preparing *chuno,* dehydrated potatoes    Right: A market in La Paz

48

# 21

# IN WHICH COUNTRY IS "SUCRE" THE MAIN CURRENCY UNIT?

*"Sucre" is the name of the currency in Ecuador. But cane sugar, too, is one of the main sources of wealth in this little, highly agricultural country.*

Crossed by the equator, as its name suggests, Equador was part of the Incan Empire and did not separate from Peru until 1830. The greater part of its resources today come from the coastal plain, which is humid and very hot all year. In addition to sugarcane, bananas, coffee, and cocoa are grown, and the virgin forest supplies balsa, appreciated by model airplane makers for its lightness. Kapok fiber is also gathered, as well as palm leaves, which are woven to make the so-called "panama" hats, popular for many years in Europe and the United States as protection from the sun.

But the hot, humid climate of the coastal plains is hard to tolerate, and three-quarters of Ecuadorians, from 11 million in a country the size of Colorado, prefer to live in the mountains of the great Andean cordillera. Even though communications, long provided by mule or llama caravans, remain difficult, and though the land is poorer, the air is healthier. The capital, Quito, is located there. At an altitude of around 9,350 feet (2,850 m) it has a year-round climate comparable to the freshness of a North American spring.

Top: Banana sellers in Ecuador
Bottom left: A coffee factory in Ecuador
Bottom right: Ecuadoran money

# 22

# WHERE WAS "EL DORADO"?

According to legend, every year the Chibcha Indians of Colombia honored the goddess of Lake Guatavita by throwing into the lake large amounts of gold and emeralds while their ruler, dusted with gold, floated on a raft. Thus arose the myth of El Dorado, the "Golden City" that the Spanish sought in vain.

Though the silver, lead, copper, and zinc mines of Peru, Chile, and especially Bolivia are among the richest in the world, gold is less abundant in the Andes. Only a few mines are really cost-effective to work.

The Indians learned to get rid of gold hunters by pointing them in the direction of fabulous treasures "over that way, beyond the horizon." But they were defenseless against colonists who came later to set up plantations on the warm, humid Colombian coast or in the deep valleys that separate the Andean chains. Bananas, then Colombian coffee, appreciated worldwide, and petroleum, became the country's principal riches.

However, unjust treatment inflicted by large landowners in Colombia on blacks, people of mixed race, and Indians who worked the land resulted in flare-ups of violence that are far from over. Drug cartels have been able to grow, in part because they provide jobs for people who have no other outlets. In its attempts to stem this violence and improve the economy, the Colombian government has been trying to develop the country's mineral resources rather than rely so heavily on its export of coffee. They have also made great efforts to bring the leaders of the drug cartels to trial.

Top: The Caravi mine, the tin center of Bolivia
Bottom: The gold museum in Lima

# 23

# WHAT IS COCA?

The Indians of the Andes have long been familiar with coca, whose leaves they chew to alleviate fatigue. But today, a hard drug is extracted from coca: cocaine, which is a major component of drug trafficking.

A man chewing a dried coca leaf

The Indians gave the name "coca" to a shrub something like a grapevine, whose small leaves are chewed with lime, after being dried in the sun. The coca leaves have the property of helping the body combat not only fatigue and altitude sickness but also pain and infection.

The peasants of the Andes cultivated this medicinal plant carefully. Europeans also learned to appreciate this remedy, while North Americans made a drink that became popular: coca-cola, a mixture of sparkling water, sugar, and coca. Westerners came up with the idea of using cocaine, a powder extracted from coca, not as a tonic remedy but as a hard drug. Those who use it generally find they can no longer do without it. Their dependency drives them to get the drug no matter what the cost.

Attracted by huge profits from this market, criminals and drug traffickers encourage or force poor mountain peasants to farm coca on an industrial scale. They then distribute this poison worldwide through the "Medellín cartel" in Colombia, as well as certain revolutionary movements like the "Shining Path" in Peru. Immensely rich, these criminals and their activities proliferate, despite the joint efforts of police forces all over the world. However, the president of Peru, Alberto Fujimori, was successful in capturing the leader of the "Shining Path" in 1992. This appears to have ended the movement's effort to seize power.

Bottom right:
Coca, the sacred plant of the Indians

Bottom left: Preparing ingredients for the Khallawayos healers in the Charazani Valley

# 24

# WHAT ARE REEDS FROM LAKE TITICACA USED FOR?

To make their canoes, the Aymara Indians use the reeds that grow in abundance on the banks of Lake Titicaca. Piled together, the reeds form veritable floating islands that can support huts.

As the "island" rots away from underneath, new layers of fresh reeds, called *totoras*, are added on top, renewing the ground on which the next crop will be grown.

Titicaca is an immense lake, with tides and sometimes heavy storms when the icy Andean wind is blowing. Roughly the size of one-fourth of Maryland, and shared by Peru and Bolivia, it is located at an altitude of 12,507 feet (3,812 m) in the heart of the altiplano. The vast high plain in the center of the Andean cordillera has long been inhabited by the Aymara Indians, in spite of its rugged climate and rarefied air.

Desert country over the whole of its southern part, this region has probably been inhabited for over 10,000 years and contains traces of the temple of Tiahuanaco, dating from a time far more ancient than that of the Inca. The Inca were so impressed by such an edifice that they adopted the technique used to build it, even asserting that their supreme god, Inti, and the founding kings of the Incan dynasty as well, were all born from the waters of Lake Titicaca.

Left: A reed boat carrying a young Aymara fisherman
Right: A village built completely of reeds in Lake Titicaca

# 25

# HOW DID BOLIVIA GET ITS NAME?

There are only two countries in the world that have been named for a man: Colombia, named in memory of Christopher Columbus, and Bolivia, in homage to Simón Bolívar, who freed South America from Spanish domination.

Born in 1783 into a wealthy Venezuelan family of high rank, Bolívar had a tragic life. To forget the death of his wife, he tried to give some meaning to his life by fighting to free his country from Spanish rule.

After difficult beginnings, which brought him exile or prison several times, he was finally able to gather a small army of partisans and free "New Grenada," later organized as Gran Colombia, of which he became president in 1819. Bolívar continued his struggle for the independence of South America, Spanish at the time, and succeeded in liberating the whole continent. One of the new states was named Bolivia in his honor, in 1925.

By 1930 Gran Colombia split up into three states: Venezuela, Colombia, and Ecuador. Bolívar began to be in disfavor. Disputes among his earliest companions, and rivalries among the countries that owed him their independence, made **Simón Bolívar** regret that he had pursued the cause of liberation with such dedication. Consumed by disillusionment and grief, this great leader renounced any official role. He died a recluse at 47, never guessing that he would hold a place of honor in the history of South America.

La Paz, capital of Bolivia, seen from the outskirts

# 26

# WHERE IS THE "RICH HILL"?

Cerro Rico, the "rich hill," is the Spanish name given by the conquistadores to the Potosi silver ore deposits in Bolivia. It is still one of the country's principal riches.

Though the silver mines, worked since Incan times, are almost exhausted today, the subsoil of this part of the high plateau contains many other sought-after metals, notably, tin, lead, zinc, and antimony.

That is why the puna, or Andean steppe, an arid region of saltwater lakes and meager pastures, is fairly well populated just the same. There, too, the Spanish colonists and their descendants, with even more brutality than elsewhere, seized the mineral resources, while the Aymara Indians, the major group in Bolivia, were reduced to working in the mines in very harsh conditions for meager wages. Thus in Bolivia, Indian revolts against the Spanish occupiers were the most frequent and the most violently repressed.

As in Peru, the fall in ore prices on the world market plunged the country into crisis, reducing the poorer Bolivians to abject poverty. Finding no more work in the mines, many now live in shantytowns on the outskirts of La Paz, the highest capital city in the world at about 12,000 feet (3,660 m) above sea level. A poor, under-developed country, Bolivia has lost a large part of its former territory in wars with its more powerful neighbors, Paraguay and Chile. Chile, by seizing the Atacama Desert, cut Bolivia off from the sea, more profoundly isolating a country already lagging in its development.

Left: Altiplano: gathering tin
Right: Crushing the tin

# 27

# WHICH IS THE MOST STRIKING OF ALL DESERTS?

*The Atacama Desert in the northern third of Chile, with a salty soil that is even sulfurous in places, has a more or less permanent drought.*

othing grows in this region, making the huge open-cast copper mines one of the country's principal resources.

The Chuquicamata mine, the largest open-cast mine in the world, produces over 2,000 metric tons of copper a day, 13 percent of total world production.

This ore-rich desert also has gold, silver, and iron mines, not to mention places where salt and saltpeter which make the region so inhospitable, are mined.

At the foot of the permanently snowcapped volcanoes sparkle the white, yellow, and even black sands of the strange Valley of the Moon, which is supposed to be haunted by spirits. It is one of the most amazing sights on earth, especially when, at a turn in the road, one sees the faulous Tatio geyser field.

Top: The Atacama Desert
Right: The geyser in Tatio

# WHICH IS THE WORLD'S LONGEST COUNTRY?

On the map of South America it is easy to recognize Chile; a strip of land 2,650 miles (4,265 km) long, less than 65 miles (427 km) wide, one of the narrowest countries in the world. It lies between the Andes and the Pacific Ocean.

C hile is a country of extreme diversity, ranging from the extremely dry deserts in the north to the conifer forests in the south that signal the proximity of the Antarctic.

There is always mountain country nearby with its mineral wealth, freshwater streams, and the opportunity to practice snow sports at any time of year. But there are inherent dangers, too, such as the earthquakes that regularly damage the towns. Chile was long cut off from its neighbors by impassable summits. Arica Pass, used to get to La Paz, the capital of Bolivia, by train, reaches an altitude of about 14,500 feet (4,420 m). So its inhabitants turned seaward, to ports like Valparaiso.

More closely linked to Europe (especially Germany, England, and Italy) than to the rest of Latin America, Chile is the most modern, industrialized, and "western" of the Andean countries. It is also the country where the indigenous population is weakest in numbers: of the Araucana Indians, who so valiantly resisted the conquistadores, there are now only 130,000 surviving, driven back into the cold southern regions. The 13 million Chileans of Spanish origin live mainly in the beautiful Santiago Valley, whose Mediterranean climate makes it possible to raise animals and cultivate wheat, fruit, and grapevines.

Top: The mountains in Chile
Bottom: Santiago

# 29

# HOW DID THE GALAPAGOS ISLANDS GET THEIR NAME?

In 1535, the first Spaniard to sail along the 13 volcanic islands of this archipelago, off Ecuador, forgot to name them. He merely noted that they were home to huge "galápagos," the Spanish word for tortoises.

For a long time sailors, misled by the changing currents that circulate among the islands and impressed by the wildness and ragged outlines of these volcanic lands, believed that the islands moved. They nicknamed them the "Enchanted Isles." That view was not shared by the colonists who tried to settle there. Despite the fertility of the soil in places, loneliness ended up discouraging most pioneers from America or Europe.

Though only a few people lived on the islands, the giant tortoises that had given their name to the archipelago barely escaped extermination. They were victims of passing seamen who hunted them for their meat, also of dogs and pigs introduced by men. These animals, having reverted to the wild state, ate the tortoises' eggs and young.

The most famous visitor to the islands was probably Charles Darwin, who came with a scientific expedition from the H.M.S. *Beagle* in 1835. Today, Ecuador permits only a few infrequent visits to the archipelago, now a wildlife sanctuary. Seabirds from the South Pole, tortoises, and **iguanas**, those impressive reptiles, are kings there now.

Top: A macaw    Bottom: The giant Galapagos turtle

# 30

# WHERE DID THE GIANT STATUES ON EASTER ISLAND COME FROM?

The Dutch explorer Jacob Roggeveen, the first European to disembark on Easter Island, found nothing there except colossal stone figures and a few local people, who were quite incapable of erecting them. He thought the statues were perhaps the handi-work of mysterious "visitors."

Survivors of a remarkable people, the Easter Islanders are believed to have been American Indians or Polynesians who came in 400 A.D. to colonize this fertile island in the Pacific Ocean, 2,300 miles (3,700 km) off the coast of Chile.

Highly civilized, they invented the only writing known at the time in that part of the world. They also carved out of volcanic rock the *moai*, gigantic busts topped with huge red stone "hats" and dedicated to their ancestors, the largest of which is nearly 40 feet (12 m) tall and weighs 83 metric tons. Shortly before the discovery of the island by Roggeveen on Easter Sunday in 1722, food began to run short, and as a result of internal wars and famine, the culture declined. The Easter Islanders overturned the statues, which no longer had any religious meaning for them.

The population of 12,000 islanders declined because of slave traders and smallpox. The present handful of survivors know less about the refined culture of their ancestors than scholars who, intrigued by the mystery, have devoted their research to the amazing history of this island.

The *moai* on Eastern Island

# A

**ANTEATER :** mammal that can grow to 8 feet (2.4 m) long, whose toothless mouth is armed with a narrow, viscous tongue that is used to capture the ants on which it feeds.

**AQUEDUCT :** a construction designed to collect and direct water from one place to another.

**ARMADILLO (NINE-BANDED OR PEBA) :** a small mammal from South America whose body is covered with corneous plates and that can roll up into a ball.

**ASTRONOMICAL :** related to the observation of the stars.

**AZTEC :** American Indians who ruled an empire in Mexico from the 1400s to the 1500s, until conquered by the Spaniards in 1521. They had one of the most advanced civilizations in the Americas.

# C

**CHAVIN :** culture that derives its name from the temple ruins discovered near Chavin at an altitude of about 10,500 feet (3,200 m). Between 850 and 200 B.C., Chavin was a religious center that attracted crowds of pilgrims from neighboring valleys.

**CHIMU :** a people who in the twelfth century, gained control over a large part of the territory of present-day Peru, thanks to flawless military organization. They built Chanchan, which became their capital in the thirteenth century. They imposed a central government on those they conquered, and subjected them to the payment of costly tribute. Faced with a desert environment, they repaired the canals and aqueducts built by the Mochica a few centuries earlier. Capable of metal craft but poor at ceramics, the Chimu mass-produced many useful objects and mastered various gold-working techniques.

**CHINCHILLA :** a small rodent that lives in Peru and Chile. Its pearl-gray fur is extremely valuable.

**CHOLERA :** a very serious epidemic disease characterized by diarrhea, vomiting, cramps, and prostration.

**CONQUISTADORES :** The name given to the Spanish adventurers who set out to conquer America.

# D

**DERBY :** a stiff felt hat with a narrow brim and dome-shaped crown, this fashion was imported to Continental Europe from England, where the hats were known as "bowlers," and thus made its way to South America, to be adopted by the women of an Andean Indian tribe.

# E

**EL DORADO :** in Spanish this means *the gilded*. It refers to a legendary place of enormous wealth.

# F

**FRANCISCO PIZARRO :** Spanish conquistador (1475–1541) who undertook the conquest of Peru for the Spanish crown.

# G

**GUANO :** a substance made of the accumulations of seabird droppings, which is a nitrogen-rich fertilizer. These birds are now protected by the government.

# H

**HERNANDO CORTÉS :** Spanish conquistador (1485–1547). Leading an expedition to Mexico, he landed in 1519 in what is now Veracruz, then marched to Tenochtitlan, the Aztec capital on the site of Mexico City.

**HIRAM BINGHAM :** an explorer and U.S. senator (1875–1956) who located the Incan capital of Vilcabamba in Machu Picchu in 1911.

# I

**IGUANA :** saurian reptile of tropical America that looks like a large-sized lizard with a dorsal crest.

**INCA :** the name given to the rulers of the Quechua people of Peru, whose empire dominated the region from the middle of the fifteenth century until 1532.

**INCAN EMPIRE :** Began developing in the fifteenth century. Its structure, its tightly planned economic system, described by some as "socialist," its solar religion, and its complex governmental hierarchy, make it one of the most original states in human history.

**INTI :** the sun god in the Inca religion, believed to be an ancestor of the Inca and represented in human form.

# K

**KAPOK :** a plant fiber that is impermeable, rot-proof, and very light, consisting of fine silky hairs that cover the seeds of a silk-cotton (ceiba) tree.

# M

**MACHU PICCHU :** now an archeological site, it sits on a mountain 8,000 feet (2,400 m) high in the Andes. The Spanish conquistadores were unaware of this citadel, which was not discovered until 1911 by Hiram Bingham.

**MOCHICA :** settled on the northern coast of Peru, the Mochica extended their influence toward the neighboring oases and fertile valleys. In the fifth century they dominated a territory nearly 190 miles (306 km) long. Wall paintings and ceramics made by their potters are like living picture books, depicting Mochican religious life.

# P

**PARACA :** a culture on the southern coast of Peru that began to develop in the fifth century B.C. The Paraca are best known for the huge necropolises where hundreds of deceased were buried. These were funeral villages with underground houses containing remarkable pottery and elegant fabrics in shimmering colors. The quality of these fabrics and the richness of their decorations reveal the astonishing technical mastery achieved in the Amerindian world.

**PRE-COLUMBIAN :** used primarily in reference to Central and South America, the term relates to their histories and civilizations before the arrival of Christopher Columbus.

**PUNA :** group of high plateaus (altiplano) in the Andes located at about 13,000 feet (4,000 m) in Peru and western Bolivia, rising above the Chaco plains. In these high grasslands animal husbandry (cattle and sheep) is practiced on an extensive scale. This is the domain of Indian herdsmen.

# Q

**QUECHUA :** the most important ethnic community in the Andes. The Quechua are made up of a number of groups, organized into chiefdoms whose unity rests mainly on language, and brought together in the sixteenth century under the domination of the Inca.

# S

**SEISMIC :** related to earthquakes: shocks, sudden deformations of the earth's crust that constitute an earthquake.

**SIMÓN BOLÍVAR :** South American liberator (1783–1830) who won independence for Bolivia, Colombia, Ecuador, Peru, and Venezuela. He wrote the constitution of Bolivia, named in his honor.

**SMALLPOX :** a serious, contagious disease, characterized by a generalized eruption of red spots that develop into pustules and leave permanent scars.

# V

**VIRACOCHA :** the most important Incan god, he created nature.

| Western Civilization | | Andean Civilization |
|---|---|---|
| | **B.C.** | |
| Construction of the first great pyramid (2589) | **3000** | The most ancient ceramics in South America at Puerto Hormiga, Colombia, and in Ecuador (3000) |
| Bronze Age in Europe (1700–800) | **2000** | Chavin culture in northern Peru (c. 1200–300) |
| Construction of Parthenon (447–438) | **1000** | Paraca culture in Peru (800–200) The dead and offerings are wrapped up to make *fardos*, mummy bundles. Nazca geoglyphs (200) |
| Destruction of Pompei (79) Advent of Attila (434) | **0** | Mochica civilization (c. 600) |
| Birth of Mohammed (570) | **500** | Tiahuanaco culture (500–1000) Cultural influence extends to northern Chile and northwestern Argentina |
| Independence of Portugal (1128) Start of Hundred Years' War (1339) First voyage of Columbus (1492) | **1000** | Chimu civilizations (1200–1450) with the capital Chanchan on the north coast of Peru Founding of Incan Empire by Pachacutec Yupanqui (1438–1471) |
| Lifetime of Michelangelo (1475–1564) | **1500** | First voyage of Pizarro, who followed the coastline of Peru (1524) Execution of the Inca Atahualpa (1533) Founding of Lima (1535) |
| Jamestown is settled (1609) | **1600** | |
| Daniel Defoe writes *Robinson Crusoe* (1719) Lifetime of Mozart (1756–1791) Georgia, the last American colony, is established (1733) | **1700** | Creation of the Viceroyalty of New Grenada, comprising the territories of Venezuela, Colombia, and Ecuador (1739) |
| The United States issues the Monroe Doctrine (1823) Spanish-American War (1898)—The United States takes control of Cuba and Puerto Rico | **1800** | End of the Spanish-Portuguese colonial empire in Latin America. Death of Simón Bolívar (1830) |
| The United States adopts the Big Stick Policy (1903) First World War (1914–1918) First man walks on the moon (1969) | **1900 A.D.** | Opening of the Panama Canal (1914) Victory of the Cuban revolution under the leadership of Fidel Castro (1959) President Carter signs the Panama Canal Treaty, giving control of the canal to the Panamanians by the end of the century (1978) |

# SOUTH AMERICA

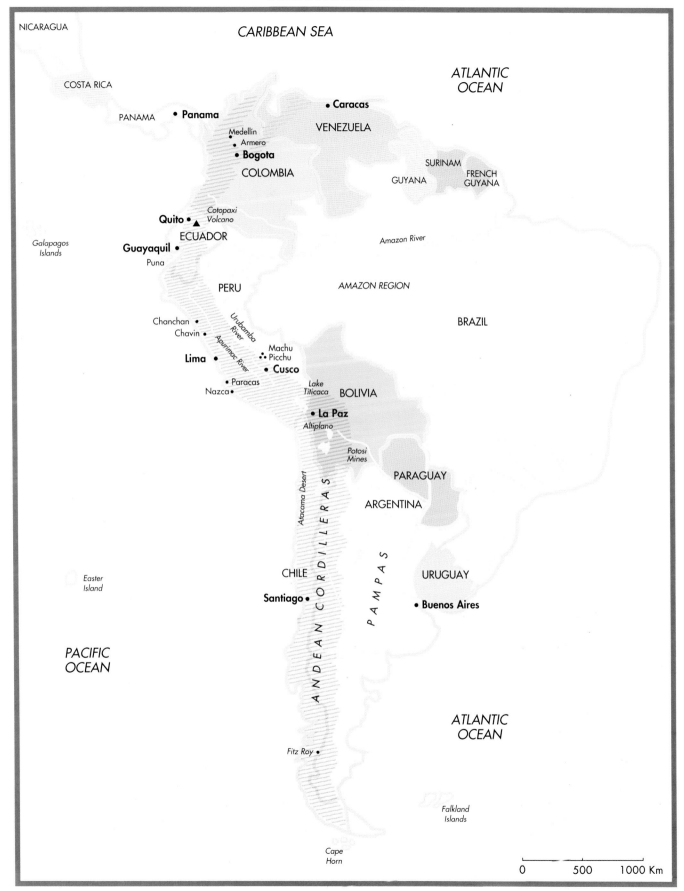

NICARAGUA

CARIBBEAN SEA

ATLANTIC
OCEAN

COSTA RICA

PANAMA    • **Panama**

• **Caracas**

VENEZUELA

Medellín •
• Armero
• **Bogota**

COLOMBIA

SURINAM

GUYANA    FRENCH
GUYANA

Cotopaxi
Volcano
**Quito** •  ▲

ECUADOR

Galapagos
Islands

**Guayaquil** •

Puna

PERU

Amazon River

AMAZON REGION

BRAZIL

Chanchan •

Chavin •

Urubamba
River

Machu
Picchu

**Lima** •

Apurímac River

**Cusco**

• Paracas

Nazca •

Lake
Titicaca

BOLIVIA

• **La Paz**

Altiplano

Potosí
Mines

PARAGUAY

ARGENTINA

Atacama Desert

ANDEAN CORDILLERAS

P A M P A S

Easter
Island

CHILE

URUGUAY

**Santiago** •

• **Buenos Aires**

PACIFIC
OCEAN

ATLANTIC
OCEAN

Fitz Roy •

Falkland
Islands

Cape
Horn

0    500    1000 Km

## PERU
Capital : Lima. Area : 496,225 sq. miles (1,285,216 km²). Population (1993 est.) : 22,889,000.

# index

## A

| | |
|---|---|
| Agriculture | 41, 49, 51, 53 |
| Alpaca | 40, 41 |
| Altiplano | 57 |
| Andes | 10, 11, 38, 39, 57 |
| Aqueducts | 23, 70 |
| Araucana Indians | 37, 65 |
| Astronomical calendar | 15 |
| Atacama Desert | 61, 62, 63 |
| Atalhualpa | 19, 33 |
| Aymara | 37, 57 |
| Aztec | 17, 70 |

## B

| | |
|---|---|
| Bolívar, Simón | 59 |
| Bolivia | 35, 43, 57, 58, 59, 61 |
| Bingham, Hiram | 25 |

## C

| | |
|---|---|
| Chanchan | 17 |
| Chavin | 17, 70 |
| Chimu | 17, 70 |
| Chinchilla | 13, 70 |
| *Chullo* | 41 |
| Climate | 46, 47, 51, 57 |
| Chile | 61, 64, 65 |
| Coca | 54, 55 |
| Condor | 12, 13 |
| Colombia | 37, 59 |
| Conquistadores | 30, 31, 70 |
| Cordillera | 10, 11 |
| Cortés | 31, 70 |
| Cusco | 17, 22, 23, 32 |

## D

| | |
|---|---|
| Dance | 42, 43 |
| Derby hats | 41, 70 |

## E

| | |
|---|---|
| Easter Island | 68, 69 |
| Ecuador | 37, 50, 51, 59 |
| El Dorado | 31, 52, 53 |
| El Niño | 46, 47 |

## G

| | |
|---|---|
| Galapagos Islands | 66, 67 |
| Geoglyphs | 15 |
| Gold | 31, 52, 53 |
| Guano | 29, 44, 45, 70 |
| Guinea pig | 13, 39 |

## H

| | |
|---|---|
| Huayna Capac | 19, 33 |
| *Huaynos* | 43 |

## I

| | |
|---|---|
| Inca | 18, 19, 20, 21, 23, 26, 27, 28, 29, 32, 33, 34, 35, 37, 70 |

## L

| | |
|---|---|
| La Paz | 61, 65 |
| Lima | 45 |
| Llama | 13, 39, 40, 41 |

## M

| | |
|---|---|
| Machu Picchu | 23, 24, 25, 71 |
| Maya | 17 |
| Mining | 53, 60, 61, 63 |
| Mochica | 17, 71 |
| Musical instruments | 42, 43 |

## N

| | |
|---|---|
| Nazca | 14, 15 |

## O

| | |
|---|---|
| Olmec | 17 |

## P

| | |
|---|---|
| Pachacutec | 18, 19, 23 |
| Paraca | 17, 71 |
| Peru | 31, 35, 45, 46, 47, 57, 59 |
| Pizarro | 17, 19, 32, 33 |
| Potatoes | 39, 48, 49 |
| Pre-Columbian peoples | 17, 71 |
| Priests | 21, 33, 34, 35 |

## Q

| | |
|---|---|
| Quechua | 21, 29, 31, 33, 37, 71 |
| Quito | 51 |

## R

| | |
|---|---|
| Religion | 21, 34, 35 |

## S

| | |
|---|---|
| Smallpox | 33, 69, 71 |
| Sucre, Sugar | 49, 50, 51 |

## T

| | |
|---|---|
| Temple of the Sun | 32, 33 |
| Titicaca, Lake | 56, 57 |

## V

| | |
|---|---|
| Venezuela | 59 |
| Vicuña | 13, 40, 41 |

## bibliography

### PERU AND THE ANDEAN COUNTRIES, FOR READERS FROM 7 TO 77

Andrews, Michael.
*The Flight of the Condor.*
Boston: Little Brown & Company, 1982.

Bateman, Penny.
*Aztec and Incas.*
New York: Franklin Watts, 1988.

Gordon, Cyrus.
*Before Columbus.*
New York: Crown, 1971.

Hadingham, Evan.
*Lines to the Mountain Gods: Nazcas
and the Mysteries of Peru.*
New York: Random House, 1992.

Jacobsen, Karen.
*Chile.*
Chicago: Children's Press, 1991.

Kendall, Ann.
*Everyday Life of the Incas.*
New York: Dorsett Press, 1973.

Lepthern, Emilie.
*Ecuador.*
Chicago: Children's Press, 1986.

Marrin, Albert.
*Pizzaro and the Conquest of Peru.*
New York: Atheneum, 1989.

McKissack, Pac.
*The Inca.*
Chicago: Children's Press, 1985.

Morrison, Marion.
*Indians of the Andes.*
Vero Beach, Florida: Rourke Publications, 1987.

Morrison, Marion.
*Colombia.*
Chicago: Children's Press, 1990.

Mosely, Michael.
*The Incas and Their Ancestors.*
New York: Thames & Hudson, 1992.

Rogers, Barbara.
*Peru.*
Milwaukee: Gareth Stevens Publishing, 1992.

**PHOTO CREDITS**

All the photographs were taken by Jacques Cornet, except the following:

Cover: Michel Drachoussoff
–p. 11 (upper and lower right), p. 13 (top), p. 17 (lower right),
    p. 37 (bottom), p. 41 (top and lower right), p. 43, p. 47 (lower right),
    p. 51, p. 53 (top), p. 55, p. 59, p. 61: Michel Drachoussoff
    –p. 19, p. 31 (left), p. 53 (bottom): Gerard Civet.
    –p. 29: Royal Museums of Art and History, Brussels
    –p. 31 (lower right), p. 45, p. 67 (bottom): Luc Giard
    –p. 47 (top and bottom): P. Mathe
    –p. 63, p. 65: Alain Mahuzier
    –p. 69: C. Bages

Titles in the *Tintin's Travel Diaries* series:

*Africa*
*The Amazon*
*China*
*Egypt*
*India*
*Peru*
*Russia*
*The United States*